Keeping your Marriage Vows Alive through the Seasons and the Storms

I STILL SAY, *I Do*

SHIREEN SPENCER
with Che Spencer

I STILL SAY I DO
Copyright © 2020 by Shireen Spencer with Che Spencer

All rights reserved. Neither this publication nor any part of this publication may be reproduced or transmitted in any form or by any means, electronic or mechanical, including photocopying, recording or any information storage and retrieval system, without permission in writing from the author.

Unless otherwise indicated, all scriptures taken from the Holy Bible, New International Version®, NIV®. Copyright © 1973, 1978, 1984, 2011 by Biblica, Inc.™ Used by permission of Zondervan. All rights reserved worldwide. www.zondervan.com The "NIV" and "New International Version" are trademarks registered in the United States Patent and Trademark Office by Biblica, Inc.™ Scripture taken from the New King James Version®. Copyright © 1982 by Thomas Nelson. Used by permission. All rights reserved.

ISBN: 978-1-4866-1809-5
eBook ISBN: 978-1-4866-1810-1

Word Alive Press
119 De Baets Street Winnipeg, MB R2J 3R9
www.wordalivepress.ca

Cataloguing in Publication information can be obtained from Library and Archives Canada.

Marriage is under fire today like never before, so learning to embrace and navigate the challenges we will encounter in our marriages is essential to the health and success of our futures together. Shireen Spencer, along with her husband Che, share from their story with candid insight and wisdom, giving us hope that we too can overcome the seasons and storms we will face as we stay true to God and our marriage vows.

—John and Helen Burns
Pastors at Relate Church, Vancouver, B.C.
International teachers, speakers, and authors
Television hosts of *Sex, Love and Relationships*

You will love the passion, authenticity, and vulnerability of Shireen and Che Spencer in this helpful book, *I Still Say "I Do!"* Don't miss out on their grounded and practical message.

—Drs. Les and Leslie Parrott
#1 New York Times-bestselling authors of *Saving Your Marriage Before It Starts*

An inspiring story from an inspiring couple! The chapters of the book—like the chapters of their life—are infused with biblical wisdom, the practice of prayer, thoughtful teaching and humour.

In *I Still Say I Do* Che and Shireen not only tell their marriage story, they share the wisdom that comes out of their story. Che and Shireen give us a hopeful picture of what can be built through the ups and downs of life when two people honour their vows, their God and each other. The lessons learned, the marriage principles and the truth from God's word woven into this book will offer hope and encouragement to couples on the journey to oneness.

—Neil and Sharol Josephson
Directors, FamilyLife Canada

Acknowledgements

We dedicate this book to three couples who have had a great impact on our life and marriage.

To our parents, Roy and Claire, who have celebrated fifty years of marriage and shown us how to keep working on your marriage through every season. They have shown us how to support others in marriage through prayer and being available. Thanks for your example!

As a child and into my adulthood, there was a couple whose love for each other truly blessed me. His servanthood to her and her encouragement and speech towards him is forever etched in my heart and mind. Their entire life and relationship mentored me. Mr and Mrs. Eric and Dolly Wong, you are forever treasured in my heart. I love and miss you. I tell my husband and children about what your life taught me! Your legacy lives on and is not forgotten.

Morris and Rose's love was inviting and inclusive. They were always warm and welcoming. Their relationship was filled with laughter and fun. Their commitment was lived out "till death do us part." Their love was simple yet very strong. The way they served each other consistently with grace and joy was an example to us all. Thank you, Uncle Morris and Aunt Rose, for the legacy and memories that your marriage has forever left in our hearts. We love you. We miss you, uncle.

Last but not least, we give thanks to God. Our marriage is filled with strength and joy, adventure and excitement because of You! Our love is Your love poured into our lives, which we get the privilege of sharing with each other. Thank You!

Introduction

In each challenging season of life, we have been able to see our vows at work. We have held each other physically, emotionally, mentally, and spiritually. The most important gift we've given each other is holding one another in prayer. We've been through many "for better or for worse" moments but have found that we were each other's "better" gift in those moments—and that made things better. We have looked back on painful times and can honestly say that our love and faith in God has made us rich.

Our most difficult times have been lived in the tension and suspension of the vow "in sickness and in health." This book focuses on what we did that helped us stay in a place of strength and victory during those seasons.

We have learned that just because life can be difficult doesn't mean we have to become difficult people. When we pray to and praise God, our actions reflect God's heart and love. With a focus on God, joy remains in the marriage.

One
"I Do" Love You

My husband and I have only been married seventeen years, yet it feels like forever! It's a good forever, though, not the kind that's long and hard.

During this time, we've had to navigate many storms. Some of the events during our marriage have been especially hard, yet our marriage has been a joy. With God's help, we have been able to enjoy our relationship—not weaken our marriage, but grow in strength. We have grown *together*. This has been God's gift to us.

But it has also been a daily choice. In fact, I think the choice was made before we even got married. Making the choice to enjoy each other and face the journey together when problems presented themselves was easy. We had to choose love and commitment before we said our vows. We had no idea what life would bring us, but we did know that whatever came we would continue to live with each other and for each other, with God's help.

We have so many stories! I can only share a few. I hope I share ones that will inspire you to know that, no matter the difficulty, you can remain strong in marriage through the seasons and the storms.

Two
An Amazing First Date

Our first date was a memorable one for many reasons. I'm not sure which part is more etched in our memories, since we laugh about the whole thing. We should have known that this date would be a foretelling of the journey our marriage would take! It has certainly been a crazy seventeen-year adventure! Where do I begin?

I didn't know where Che was taking me, but I knew I wanted to go. So when he called to ask if I could pick him up instead of him coming to get me, I didn't hesitate to say yes. I'm sure my mother wasn't pleased, since she hadn't really met him and is a very traditional woman. He should have come to my home to meet me.

I wasn't worried in the least about going to his home, although I did wonder why he'd suggested the change. I knew I would find out soon enough. The ease I had with Che could only be explained by saying it was, and still is, a God thing!

After I pulled up to his home, I don't remember if I knocked on the door or if he met me outside. When your heart is excited about who you're about to spend time with, those details get missed, although I'm otherwise a very detailed person in many areas of my life.

I only remember that he drove my car. His remained in the driveway and couldn't be driven—not because it didn't work, he said, but because he was being a gentleman.

I didn't find out until we were sitting in the restaurant what had happened before the date. It truly is funny, yet I don't think it was the funniest part of our evening.

You'll have to decide.

Che had been bringing lunches to work in order save money. However, that day he'd realized that one of those lunches had been left in the car somewhere and had gone bad… really bad! He could smell it but hadn't been able to track down the source until it was too late.

So apparently we hadn't been able to take his car for our first date because the smell was just that horrible. I'm thankful he chose to be humble and ask to use my car.

We had a nice dinner, truly enjoying our conversation and the food. We both wanted to go see a movie after, but since our conversation was going so well we missed our window of opportunity. It would have been too late to see a different showing, so we tried to figure out something else to do next.

We decided to go for a walk. That should have been easy enough, since it would keep the conversation going. It would also be romantic. A walk is always a nice addition to a date, right?

Allergies had never come up in our conversation, but they did make their way into our date night. To say the least, they have remained a big part of our marriage! It was springtime, and the trees and flowers were just starting to show signs of life. It had been a very warm, sunny day, and when night fell the atmosphere was perfect. Picture perfect.

Well, I love the beauty of nature, but it doesn't like me at all! As the buds come to life, my life feels like it's beginning to end.

As we walked and talked, my embarrassment began. First there were the watery eyes, followed by the swelling, and soon thereafter the snorting. Yes, I began to snort! Then came the congestion.

We walked by his home in search of an allergy pill, because neither of us wanted the evening to end. We were doing all we could to save it!

I'm not a very good pill swallower, so that was a comedy show.

We then sat on the couch and said nothing. But the silence was comfortable, and it said everything. This same silence has continued to be comfortable and has spoken loudly of the love we have for each other throughout our marriage thus far. We should have known then that we were in for an adventure of a marriage!

Long before our first date, I had anticipated it. When I saw Shireen for the first time, I knew she was someone special. She had said no to meeting me once before, when she didn't yet know who I was. A common friend had told her that I was interested. So I had to leave it up to God to bring us together, which thankfully He did.

I wasn't going to let a spoiled lunch rotting in my car ruin our first time out together. My only option had been to have her come pick me up. So I called her, anticipating total honesty and transparency, and then planned to tell her what had happened when I saw her in person. For the moment, I just had to make sure our date still went forward.

She was so easy-going on the date, and we had already shared a lot of laughs. This was just going to be one more! By now you've read Shireen's version of the story, so you know the night was filled with more than just one thing to laugh at.

I knew then that life with Shireen wasn't going to be easy, but still so much fun. I planned on making sure to take this journey and enjoy it for as long as I could. I'm so grateful for our first date. I give thanks to God for the many more we have had since then.

Three
To Love and to Cherish

We were only a week into our honeymoon when the phone call came, telling me that my grandmother was really sick and we needed to come home if I expected to see her before she passed away. We had known she was too frail to travel to our wedding, but we'd had no idea she was so sick that only a miracle could have saved her.

What a dilemma to have to deal with while trying to enjoy the honeymoon we had waited for and planned for more than a year!

We made the difficult decision to stay and end the first leg of our honeymoon as intended before returning home. God granted us favour—our family kept us posted and Grandma hung on.

While returning home, a new challenge arose. I became sick the last few days of our trip with serious vertigo. We couldn't do anything about how I was feeling, and Che had his hands full!

He could have chosen to react with frustration, and I could have chosen to react with a dependence that could have ruined it for both of us. But Che became a servant, taking very good care of me, and I tried hard to allow him to still have fun and try the things he wanted to try. He went away a few hours at a time and came back to check on me and tell me about all his adventures. Thank God it was only for two days of our trip!

On the day we left, Che took care of carrying everything and all the difficulties associated with airports while I just lay across the chairs in the lounge. I was quite the sight! Looking back, I'm surprised they allowed me on the plane in the condition I was in.

Once home, Grandma was still stable, so we decided to go on the second leg of our honeymoon—a trip to a cottage up north in Ontario. We went a few days later than planned, since I still felt sick with the vertigo and an infection.

Three days into this second part of the trip, the call came—and this time we couldn't ignore it. We had to drive to New Jersey to see Grandma.

Che was already such a good husband. Everything that had gone wrong came from my side of the family, and it could have been a very frustrating time for him. He drove the ten hours to New Jersey and spent our honeymoon taking care of me and my family's needs. What an introduction into my family!

This was the last weekend before he had to return to work, so we were back and forth in a single weekend. We returned home late Sunday night and he went to work early on Monday.

That afternoon, we got the call that Grandma had passed.

Thankfully, the funeral was going to be the next weekend, so Che worked the whole week and then drove us back to New Jersey late Friday night. We again returned home on a Sunday night only for him to go to work on Monday.

While in New Jersey, my oldest uncle was also sick in the hospital—so sick, in fact, that he didn't even know his mother had passed away and wasn't told until after the funeral. When we got home on Monday, we were called again to be told that my uncle had died.

Welcome to marriage, Che!

That following weekend, we made another trip to New Jersey to bury my uncle.

Che held me in so many ways early in our marriage. He held me physically and carried me when my body didn't have strength. He held my heart and comforted me during two major deaths in the family. He also held us in prayer.

We hoped for better days, since our lives together had started in a somewhat more challenging position than we'd expected. But whatever was coming our way, I knew I was doing life with an amazing man. Our lives were rich with grief at that moment, but also rich in love.

Our introduction to marriage was quite the whirlwind. We'd had no idea that, in just the first month of marriage, Shireen would be so sick and that we'd make three round trips to New Jersey. There was nothing I could do about it.

The timing wasn't good. But when does sickness or death ever come at a good time? It was a tiring period of our lives, but this was now my family, too. I was sad and concerned about what my employer would think, but thankfully the company supported me—which helped me to support my wife.

If the situation had been reversed, I know Shireen would have done the same for me. We were family. It was my privilege to be there for her. I love her.

Four
To Have and to Hold

Three months into our marriage, our doctors questioned whether I could have children. This resulted in us having to make many choices. Would we believe that report? Would we get bitter? What if it were true? I remember Che saying to me that this hadn't been our plan, but if this ended up happening we would still have and love each other.

We could also adopt. We both wanted children, and not having any wasn't an option for us. It was just a matter of how it was going to happen.

Yes, we really wanted them to be our own biological children, so first we focused on bringing that desire to God, who can do all things. It was in His hands anyway, so we needed to take our hands off the situation.

This took a lot of prayer, since heart issues are hard to let go of, but we made it a daily practice. We told God our desires and asked Him to show us His. We believed in His best for us, and we believed His Word. He knew our desires.

I remember the doctors telling us that we should try to see if we could have children right away. We did as the doctors instructed, adding a practical action to our prayer life. It was a lot of fun—and six months after getting married, we were expecting! What did the doctors know? Once again, it hadn't been in our plan to add to our family so soon, but it was out of our hands. We moved our focus to getting ready for the gift God was supplying!

For a while, we had thought we were entering another heart-breaking journey, but it was a short-lived season in our lives. We just had to face the possibility that life might not go as planned.

These were big, emotional issues to carry, and it could have changed us. When I reflect on those months of not knowing what would happen, we had to surrender to the Lord every day.

Che has such an easy-going personality. Very few things faze him or get him into an anxious state. He has such a calm about him. I'm the one who worries.

When we were given the bad news by the doctor, Shireen probably thought I had no feelings. I'm not usually one to show much emotion, and this time was no different.

I really didn't think much about this report. I thought to myself, why worry about it? Our only option was to pray and trust that God had a plan. That's the option I chose. The choice was simple: I let go and let God.

There was no point worrying about something we couldn't control, so I looked on the bright side: the practice of trying to create a baby was going to be a lot of fun!

Whether or not the doctors were right and we couldn't have children, I took my vows seriously. I was committed to Shireen. I was committed to us. We would face whatever we needed to face together. We would focus on God and not this problem.

We focused on what we could control, and that was to love and encourage each other. We had started as a two-person family and we might have stayed that way. We needed to enjoy, protect, cherish, and love that. We focused on being the best couple we could be, on letting God take care of our hearts, and on the greatness and bigness of our God.

It seems so simple. It may not always be easy, but it *is* simple. When we simply choose to trust God, He does the rest. He is responsible for giving His strength, His peace, His hope, and His joy. He gladly does it. If we take hold of what He has to offer us, we really can enjoy blessings we wouldn't otherwise expect to come out of difficult places.

Early in our marriage, I was able to fall more in love with my husband because of his strength and confidence in God and in us. This situation brought us closer together—and we still had a lifetime ahead of us! We had each other and we held on. Even in this "for worse" time, our love and relationship got better.

Five
For Richer or for Poorer

One day when our second son was three months old, Che had left for work only to return a few hours later. I was on maternity leave and very surprised to see him come through the door. And even more surprised to see him come home with all his belongings. He had been laid off!

We never saw it coming. With two young children at home and me off work, what were we to do? I knew then that I needed to encourage him, and that I needed to remain optimistic. He didn't need me to beat him down by asking all the questions I knew he would eventually give me the answers to. That would only create anxiety.

So I stayed quiet, controlling my attitude and personal peace. That was a choice I had to make, but it didn't come easy. I'm a person who likes to talk and process and have things figured out. I process through talking. Holding my tongue took a lot of discipline and effort, but reading Che's body language helped me to know that my normal way of reacting wasn't what he needed.

I can't change anyone, but I can work on myself. I can work on bringing a positive vibe to any situation. He needed to feel safe and valued and respected and loved, so I hugged him. I told him everything would be okay. I told him I loved him.

We didn't know it then, but this season would last nearly four years. Che couldn't find work in his field, but he also didn't really want to. He wanted to build his own company, so he went back to school and took up working for his friend's company, which brought in only inconsistent money. Thank God his schooling was a government-funded program!

God continued to provide and show us how to be creative as we waited. We stuck together and supported each other. It wasn't just Che going through this; it was *us*. It was our family, our partnership and marriage. The only thing we could control was the decision to stay focused on God and bring everything to Him in prayer. We had to choose to trust Him, so that's what we did. We made the choice and our emotions followed as we prayed and praised.

> We had to choose to trust Him, so that's what we did. We made the choice and our emotions followed as we prayed and praised.

Che is the head of our home. He is my spiritual covering. My role as his wife was, and is, to encourage him—and four years is a long time to be without employment, especially for a man. What men do plays a huge role in defining them. They feel very responsible for being the provider. He needed to know that I believed in him, that I was with him and supported him, that I was proud of him and that he wasn't letting our family down.

I felt that I needed to hold Che up in prayer—in words of encouragement and in deeds of affection. He had been there for me through hard times since the first week of our marriage, and now it was my turn.

In this season, I learned not to complain. I wanted stability and consistency, but I also saw how hard Che was trying and working to fulfill his goals. I had to give him the opportunity and time to do so. It wasn't an easy time, and my response sometimes did cause friction, but God was working on me. I was learning to trust God and Che more.

As I look back on this time in our lives, the biggest thing that stands out in my mind is the support Shireen was to me. She never made me feel bad, and she gave me space to dream. She was committed to the decisions I made. We were in this together.

Honestly, those four years weren't a walk in the park. We had heated discussions about finances and times of stress during which we craved security. Our preferred means of getting there differed, but with God's help we were able to work it out through a lot of prayer. Prayer does work.

Again, God was giving us an opportunity to live out our vows. We also realized it could have been worse! We had much to be thankful for as God continued to provide.

Many times, we had more month than money and we had to rely on family and friends. We also got creative. We did without and didn't miss much. We were still rich—with love, and with faith and the belief that we wouldn't always be in that place. We were also rich with commitment, hope, and expectation.

Six
For Better or for Worse

I used to be so frustrated by Che's easy-going nature and how well he took negative news. The funny thing is that I had fallen in love with that quality before we got married.

I always tell people that Che is my neutralizer. His calm brought peace to my life and helped me face difficult people and problems. It still does today. When Che is with me, I react in a calmer manner. But I had to learn that his calm reaction wasn't an indication of him having no thoughts or feelings towards a situation; it was just his nature. He internalized a lot while still feeling deeply.

I've been a teacher for more than twenty years. One day five years ago, the worst thing that could happen to a teacher happened to me—I was wrongfully accused of physical misconduct.

And as soon as it happened, I called Che. I was looking for his calm, the sound of his voice telling me that everything was going to be okay. He suggested that I not go home but instead call a friend, so I wouldn't be alone. He was looking for a way to hold me and support me from afar until he could do it himself. I deeply appreciated his thoughtfulness and demeanour.

His calm and quiet nature is his strength, bringing to our relationship a level of certainty and safety. When I receive this from him, I feel strongly held. Even a bad time is made better just by his presence, and I'm rich in support even during an emotionally poor time. I am kept from mental sickness and brought to emotional health because of the gift of Che's attitude and perspective. He speaks quietly, but his underlying message of love is heard loud and clear. He speaks tenderly yet with conviction.

Shireen is a strong woman. I knew she would be okay because I knew that the truth of her integrity would reveal itself. I didn't want to worry about something that I believed was going to be cleared up soon, so I focused my attention on what would build up her confidence and take her mind off of that stress. It wasn't that I didn't care, but I cared more about her than the situation.

In times like these, God shows me how we live out our vows together in partnership.

Seven
In Sickness and in Health

Even before we married, Che knew me to be a woman who had many health struggles. Allergies were the least of my problems!

After we got married, those struggles only seemed to increase. Female health issues became a problem, and I had to undergo surgeries to try to correct what was happening. We went from one issue to another. Two surgeries led me to see several specialists, and Che had to drive me all over for various treatments and consultations, hoping to find someone who could fix what kept going wrong.

Until recently, every year of our marriage had come with a health issue. Even after we got the good news that I could have children, I became sick throughout my pregnancies. Very sick. I was put on modified work and bedrest. I was nauseous and in pain every day. Smells made it worse, and most times I couldn't cook. I had cravings—strong cravings—I would send Che out to buy me what I needed. Then I wouldn't be able to eat any of it.

Che took everything well. He knew I couldn't help what was going on in my body. He just thought, *This too shall pass.*

We weren't going to be in this season forever. There was no point getting upset by temporary inconveniences.

After each of my sons were born, I had complicated deliveries and had stay for a week in the hospital. When I did return home, other complications arose and I needed healing.

Che again just served me. He stayed up with the babies or woke up to get them when they cried. He drove us to the emergency room when we had to go. He took care of us all without complaint. He changed diapers, gave baths, and became involved in every aspect of our boys' lives. He didn't wait until they were older to get involved.

Shireen always asks me how I do all this without complaint or signs of stress. I don't know what to say except that I take my vows seriously. I'm a family man, the head of the family. I must set an example.

Perhaps this comes easier to me than some men because I was raised by my mom and had a sister. Through that, I'm sure that I've learned how to be sensitive to women. I've worked inside and outside of the home without thinking of gender role divisions.

I've grown up with the attitude and perspective that we must deal with what life gives us in the best way we can. This is what Shireen gets to experience with me. I guess she's lucky, or perhaps we are both just blessed.

Perhaps Che is an anomaly! He's logical and just does what needs to be done without being upset about it. He isn't perfect, but he really is a man who serves his wife and family.

My surgeries and treatments continued every year, and the problem just kept coming. Then came one year with six surgeries!

And then came cancer. I've been through so many battles of sickness. We've spent most of our seventeen years living in the tension of the vow "in sickness and in health." Through it all, Che has been an amazing caregiver.

Since I've been the one with so many health issues, feelings of guilt have washed over me at times. I feel like I've made life quite a challenge for Che, even though it hasn't been a conscious choice. Life just happened to me… to us.

Being sick for so long hasn't been my fault, yet I have known people whose husbands haven't stayed with them or supported them through to the restoration of their health. In their hard times, their marriages suffered. In our hard times, our marriage has remained good. Che could have left, physically and emotionally, but he didn't. He had a choice.

If I knew then what I know now, that we would go through so many challenging experiences, I would still marry Shireen over and over again. The outside forces that have come our way and made life difficult weren't her choice or fault. She is still the woman I married, the woman I fell in love with.

I don't get to control what comes our way. We do the best with what we've been given and let God do the rest. Perspective is everything. We just have to keep going until it gets better. It will always get better.

Shireen's health issues had no effect on my commitment to her. That was never an issue. We were committed regardless of circumstances. I had made vows and I was going to keep them.

Keeping my vows was a question of remembering my commitment to God, myself, Shireen, and our children. I was committed to be a man of integrity and honour. I was committed to staying with and being loyal to Shireen. I was committed to my boys and being a godly example of a husband and father.

I love God. I love Shireen. She loves me. These aren't just words; they're our daily experience together.

As Che and I have reflected on the difficult pages in the story of our marriage, we've both decided that we would stay committed to some choices that have helped us. These choices were made before the challenges came and are still lived out in our daily experiences, whether good or bad.

Through these choices, God has rewarded us with peace and joy in our marriage despite the difficulties. We are far from perfect, yet we are perfect for each other because we're perfectly committed to finding God at work in our marriage, and perfectly committed to practicing good choices that will make a reality those things we want for our marriage.

Eight
The Couple that Prays Together

We have had many reasons to pray together. We prayed together before we were married and continued after. We pray on our own and with each other. It's a pillar of our relationship.

We know our relationship can only be strengthened through prayer, which is why we pray a lot—and pray long. We have prayed because we needed to and because we wanted to. Prayers have been whispered, shouted, gone from our lips to God's ears in urgency and in leisure.

Together we have built our home and love on prayer. We don't know what we would do without knowing that God listens to and answers our prayers. God heard our prayers for children, for financial provision, and for healing and recovery. He heard our prayers to grow in love.

Each of my pregnancies was a nightmare in its own way. One of my sons needed lots of doctors and instruments to encourage his entry into the world. The other required me to undergo surgery. My labour for one lasted twenty-eight hours, and the other two days. One was born with a cord around his neck and wanted to come out the wrong side first; the other went into distress and needed to be saved. I didn't get to meet one of my sons until hours after the birth, as I haemorrhaged and fell unconscious.

These situations and many others required a lot of prayer. We needed prayer to strengthen us in our weakness, to turn things around. Both births could have ended badly.

With my surgeries and various diagnoses, including the one of cancer, prayer is what carried us through. We try to approach problems first with prayer, before worry can set in. That doesn't mean we don't worry; it just means that we choose prayer, before worry can intensify in our heart and minds. We know that God is in control.

We have prayed through every difficult situation in our lives, including job loss, financial problems, health scares, and disagreements. We've prayed through the good times too. Every season of life requires the same focus on prayer because God is sovereign over the good and the bad.

Rejoice always, pray continually, give thanks in all circumstances; for this is God's will for you in Christ Jesus.
(1 Thessalonians 5:16–18)

Through prayer, we can rejoice in what God is doing and have thankful hearts in all circumstances. We are thankful that we aren't alone and haven't had to go through our challenges alone. We've only been able to remain joyful because we have done as the Scripture says: pray without ceasing. We have needed joy to love the life God has given to us, and to remind us that all is not lost.

God is good. We've stayed connected to God and each other through prayer. Our prayers have caused us to stay centred on

God and His goodness. We can live a life of joy and have a happy marriage not because of us or because everything in our lives is perfect, but because God is continually working in our lives.

Though one may be overpowered, two can defend themselves. A cord of three strands is not quickly broken. (Ecclesiastes 4:12)

We have kept God as the third strand that holds our marriage together, and prayer has helped us to do this. A godly marriage cannot survive without connection to God. Prayer is the lifeline of our marriage. It does work!

Nine
The Couple that Laughs Together

Our mouths were filled with laughter, our tongues with songs of joy. Then it was said among the nations, "The Lord has done great things for them." (Psalm 126:2)

Laughter is great medicine. It relaxes and heals. We have enjoyed laughing together.

We laugh with each other, at each other, at others, and with others. We laugh at our children and with our children. We even laugh at the enemy! We cause laughter in each other's lives. Our lives are filled with laughter.

Sometimes we're silly on purpose, just to arouse a laugh from each other. We love to share a joke we've heard or something funny we've seen online. We love to just hear each other laugh. We plan laughter and create reasons to laugh on purpose. The joy of the Lord is our strength. We've laughed when we were tired and had sleepless nights. We've found reasons to laugh through our tears and pain.

We started laughing together on our first date! We knew laughter would help strengthen us and allow us to make it through difficulties, but it's also helped us to maintain our perspective. Sometimes during disagreements we just stop, look at each other, and laugh after a statement has been said that we both realize was silly or didn't make sense. The laughter comes naturally.

Sometimes Che tells jokes or makes a funny expression of affection that eases the tension, and I can't stay mad. Laughter has truly allowed us to tackle heavy situations and conversations with a lightness only God can give. Laughter forces us to find a place of joy and peace.

With my hair growing back after chemo, it's taken on various styles all on its own. I have no control over what's happening to it. I really don't like it. From time to time, Che just looks at me and laughs, as I truly do look comical. This gets me laughing and moves me away from the seriousness of hair loss and makes me feel gratitude in my heart that it's growing back. We can laugh because funny hair is a sign of life and healing for us.

A happy heart makes the face cheerful, but heartache crushes the spirit. (Proverbs 15:13)

Ten
The Couple that Cries Together

We have had many reasons to cry on our journey of marriage. The tears have come from very deep places. They've come from places of happiness and places of sadness, from places of pain and places of comfort, in places of prayer and places of worship. We have cried together, and we have cried apart from each other.

We haven't been afraid to share our feelings through tears. Being able to cry has built intimacy between us. God has used our tears to strengthen our marriage.

I'm a very expressive person. I feel deeply and my emotions last long. Yet I also know that my tears are mine. I don't use them to manipulate.

I feel free sharing my tears with Che. He accepts them. He values them.

Che and I differ in that he doesn't wear his emotions on his sleeve like I do. But he's not afraid to show his emotions or feelings. He is not afraid to cry. We've been able to be truly strong for each other in times of tears for each other or with each other.

My own relationship with God has always been an open one where I feel comfortable and free to show different emotions. This hasn't changed since marrying Shireen. My wife has always supported and encouraged me to show whatever level of emotion I choose without being pressured. She wants me to be true to myself and always open and right with God.

I feel that God gave us emotions for a reason. I have never felt that my manhood is contingent upon how much or how little emotion I exhibit. Crying doesn't make me more or less of a man or closer or farther from God. I just want to follow the example of Christ and no one else's. When I cry or am true to myself and accept and show any given emotion, I feel free and released. I feel closer to Shireen and closer to God.

Showing true emotions is important because it lets Shireen know I'm human! As funny as this may sound, it's true. If Shireen is going to know all of me, she needs to see all of me—the good, the bad, the ugly, the hurt and the healed, the sad and the happy. Real life is messy, but the truth in the mess is beautiful when it can be shared with the person you love the most.

There are men who feel that crying isn't a male trait, yet Jesus wept. Being a man who can cry is being human. Being a man who cries because God has touched his life and heart is divine to me.

I am blessed with a man who can cry before God, and because of this I have been gifted with a man who can be sensitive to me and my needs. He is blessed with a wife who allows him to feel strong in his tears, a wife who encourages his tears as they come, a wife who doesn't let her own tears control him but bless him.

> *Those who sow with tears will reap with songs of joy. Those who go out weeping, carrying seed to sow, will return with songs of joy, carrying sheaves with them.* (Psalm 126:56)

> *He heals the brokenhearted and binds up their wounds.* (Psalm 147:3, NKJV)

> *The Lord is close to the brokenhearted and saves those who are crushed in spirit.* (Psalm 34:18)

Our lives are a testament to these verses. Releasing our tears and not holding anything back from each other or God has made space for joy. It's made space for peace, for strength, and for healing. God has used our tears to wash away what's hurt us and He has taken care of our wounds. He has used our tears to soften our hearts towards each other to see that when one of us hurts, we both do—and that has caused us to always work at being a healing vessel for each other in our marriage.

> He has used our tears to soften our hearts towards each other to see that when one of us hurts, we both do—and that has caused us to always work at being a healing vessel for each other in our marriage.

Eleven
The Couple that Is Honest About Feelings

I can remember asking Che to tell me if there was ever a time when his eyes wandered away from seeing me and if his heart has ever done the same. He thought I was crazy, but I figured it was much better to know the truth than to keep secrets from each other. And so I ask often. This keeps us both accountable.

His answer is always the same, but at least I know I can ask the question, and that I can trust him. He knows the same of me.

A wandering eye is natural. Is it wandering to notice beauty? I think it's natural to comment on another woman's looks or dress, but I believe we have to be sensitive with our partner on how we communicate those thoughts.

I respect and love Shireen. I want my thoughts and comments to be expressions of that love. I want my comments and actions to show that I respect God, myself, Shireen, and others. It's crucial that

I make sure not to cross a line—that line was created by God and also Shireen's comfort.

Shireen asking me questions just keeps us accountable and comfortable with each other. Lust should not be natural or normal. Checking up on each other like this keeps lust from setting in. The closer I am to Shireen, and to God, the easier it is to stay further away from any line that shouldn't be crossed.

Your partner needs to know what you find attractive so that they can be confident in the reasons you find them attractive. It's not about ranking or sex appeal. I believe your partner wants to know that they inspire the same reaction in you as when you recognize beauty in others—even more so, in fact!

My body has been through so many changes. Having children changes you inside and out. My surgeries have taken what was once flawless and filled it with scars… scars that tell stories of victory.

Cancer transforms a person. This was especially true for me when I went from having long hair to no hair. I wouldn't have blamed Che for wanting a different wife, even a different life. I am today not the woman he married, and for him it's very hard to have to be a constant caregiver. It's hard to be a single parent when there are physically two parents around. It's hard not to get tired, yet I'm still so very much loved.

My husband still wants me and lets me know this every day through his words and actions. I still want him and don't take for granted how much he has given up in order to take care of me. I tell him constantly how much I appreciate him and how much he has done for our family. I don't think we could ever convey too much our love for each other. We can never be too clear or too specific about the things we do for each other that make us love each other more. There just aren't enough words!

Let your speech always be with grace, seasoned with salt, that you may know how you ought to answer each one.
(Colossians 4:6, NKJV)

During a season of pain and struggle, it is so important to communicate. It's not a time to close up and run from each other. The channels must be kept open.

Of course, because we aren't perfect, there are things we haven't liked about each other. We have learned to share the truth in love. We have made it a practice to share the truths that might not be comfortable to hear. We've learned to also share these truths at times when we're getting along, when love and like coexist. We've learned to share with each other in phrases and tones that our ears will receive.

We aren't always good at this, but it's something we have sought to practice. What's most important here is that we don't keep anything from each other. Whether or not the other person wants to hear what we have to say, we have vowed to be open and honest. Knowing that this honesty comes from a place of love helps us to receive each other's words.

In our first year of marriage, we began a yearly ritual. For Christmas, we don't buy each other presents. Our gift to each other is to write a love letter of the year in review. In it, we write about what we have grown to love about each other. We share the moments that meant so much to us. We write about what we are proud of in each other. We write about what we look forward to seeing grow in each other for the next year.

Each year, we wait with excitement and anticipation to see what the other has written. We are so glad that we started this tradition. It has helped us to see how much good exists in our marriage, even in the bad times. Our yearly love letters help us to keep track of the love we have shared year-round.

We want to outwrite each other, not in word count but in the depth of the memories shared and how loved we have felt. Knowing that we will be writing about our love helps us to work at outdoing each other in expressing our love for each other every day.

Do everything in love. (1 Corinthians 16:14)

Twelve
The Couple that Lives in the Moment

At times in our marriage, we wish we could be somewhere else. We've wished many times that we weren't experiencing that which we've been given. But wishing it away doesn't make it go away. Our troubles don't go by fast, or at all. We've had to walk through our difficulties. There were no shortcuts.

Consider it pure joy, my brothers and sisters, whenever you face trials of many kinds, because you know that the testing of your faith produces perseverance. (James 1:2–3)

There have been moments in our marriage I haven't enjoyed. But I always think about how I want to remember myself handling these tough times when I get the opportunity to look back on them. So while living in these negative spaces, I try to choose to make the best decisions with what I've been given.

During these times, I just tell myself to be real. Embrace the now. Do what must be done, whether you like it or not.

I went into survival mode during Shireen's illness not just for me, but for the survival of my family. I had no other choice.

I felt he did. He could have left and walked away altogether. It would have been understandable—not acceptable, but understandable. We've seen that happen with our friends. But instead he stayed—and while he stayed, we talked. We talked about what we were feeling. We talked about decisions that we'd had to make. We talked about our fears. We talked about our joys.

There have been moments when we haven't talked, since no words needed to be spoken. Words would not have helped us in the place we found ourselves. In those moments—of miscarriages, of job loss, of sickness—we held on to each other. We sat in the pain together and let it run its course.

We also focused on what was good in each moment. We could share that we didn't like what was happening, while focusing on cheering each other up. When we were tired, we said so, and then we rested. When we didn't want something to happen, we said so and then made a choice to change it if it was in our power to do so. Other times we allowed a matter to run its course, but meanwhile we controlled our attitude and thoughts.

There have been moments during my health journeys that were very difficult for Che, especially my fight with cancer. He was frustrated, angry, and tired, having had a hard time seeing me suffer. I let him vocalize his feelings, and then I encouraged him. Of course he felt that way; he wouldn't have been human if he didn't.

He didn't always handle his frustration well, but whenever he exhibited anger I knew that it wasn't about me. It was about the situation we were both in. We have always been on the same team, and we will not be divided.

Our responses to each other could build us up or tear us down. We could bring upon ourselves more unnecessary difficulty to an already difficult situation or we could take turns bringing strength to each other. We have chosen to be builders. We have helped to build each other's faith, confidence, and focus on gratitude. Through it all, we have helped to build our marriage. At times when we've felt like we were falling apart, God was building our marriage story.

> We could bring upon ourselves more unnecessary difficulty to an already difficult situation or we could take turns bringing strength to each other. We have chosen to be builders.

Be completely humble and gentle; be patient, bearing with one another in love. Make every effort to keep the unity of the Spirit through the bond of peace. (Ephesians 4:2–3)

We made a conscious effort to be patient with each other in times when our patience could have worn thin. Prolonged sickness can put anyone on edge, and it took understanding of where each of us were in our emotions and physical state, and then intentionally and practically extending grace, to keep us moving forward, disentangled from the unnecessary trap of misunderstood emotions that could pull us away from the truth. And the truth is that we did love each other.

I don't like hospitals, so being there during Shireen's health issues were the hardest times for me. I've always had a phobia when it comes to hospitals. I tend to think that death is synonymous with hospitals—that's wrong, I know—so I'm always a little nervous when Shireen needs to visit there. Those are the times when I truly need God.

We know that the battle is the Lord's. Since we believed this to be true, we knew the Lord was fighting for us. We put on our armor and prayed and praised. We waited on the Lord and trusted Him to give us what we needed in order to face our reality.

There were times of great discomfort, but we made each other as comfortable as we could, living through our difficulties without allowing them to affect how we treated each other. We made a conscious effort to not be difficult people.

As a patient, I worked hard on my attitude to make sure Che didn't feel burdened. I focused on the goodness and strength of God. By the power of the Holy Spirit, I remained a very positive person. As Scripture fell from my lips and was implanted deep in my heart, and as worship music filled the atmosphere, God gave me a garment of joy and praise.

Che served me without complaint. He took care of the details in our home I usually took care of. He put my needs before his own, knowing I would do the same for him, but also knowing that this is what was needed. He did what he had to because it needed to be done.

Dealing with Shireen's health has been hard, but it's been that way since our first date. I draw all my patience and strength from how Shireen handles each situation. She rarely complains, and she always looks on the bright side. She is proactive with finding solutions to problems.

She doesn't let her health dominate her, which sometimes means she doesn't get enough rest. In those times, I sometimes get mad or frustrated, because in her desire to continue on with life as normally as possible she can push past her limit. Sometimes I can see it coming, and I ask her to slow down. But she doesn't. Then, lo and behold, she crashes. That's when my patience wears thin.

In our difficult moments of frustration or anger, we admitted how we felt and didn't try to avoid the situation. If we needed space, we let each other have it. If we needed to confront a situation head-on, we did so. We knew that avoidance wasn't an option for us and that we needed to work through pain to get to healing.

> *And over all these virtues put on love, which binds them all together in perfect unity.* (Colossians 3:14)

Che has said that my approach to life has made it easy for him to respond to my sicknesses. I say that it's how he took care of me that allowed me to approach each illness with a positive mindset, to work hard to make the journey as easy as I could.

We have both put the other first and been concerned with making the other happy. We both loved the Lord first, and then each other second. Our focus on this kept us unified.

Thirteen
The Couple that Has a Support System

There were always people we could call on. We had our family, our friends, our colleagues, and our church. But just because you have people you can count on doesn't mean you'll actually let yourself rely on them. Just as it takes a village to raise a child, that same village helps a marriage stay strong.

We invited the ministry of others, but that didn't come easy for me. It was a hard learning curve. I'm a very independent woman. But God wants us to operate as a body that helps and supports each other. Marriage cannot be done well without the support of others.

When I was having a miscarriage, it was a difficult time for us. We had just found out that I was expecting. I had been pregnant nearly three months without knowing it. When we found out, though, we embraced the pregnancy with great expectation and happiness. I was sure this was my baby girl.

With my other two pregnancies, I had been sick from the day of conception to the day I gave birth. For this one, I wasn't.

But the pleasant surprise quickly left us when the baby miscarried, something we hadn't expected.

We thank God that we had each other, but we also thank God that people were willing to step in to help us with our boys so that we could cry together without bringing sadness into their lives. This was a "to have and to hold" and "for better or for worse" moment in our lives. People held us both in prayer and in practical ways.

I will never forget one particular day when I was surprised by bad news at school. The vice principal pulled me aside and said something that completely blindsided me! I saw his lips moving, but it took me a while to hear clearly what he was telling me: I was being accused of physical misconduct.

The main thing I remember is that the vice principal then passed me the phone and told me I could call my husband.

"Honey, I've just been accused of physical misconduct," I told my husband. "I will be escorted out of school and sent home."

I walked to my car and sat there for what seemed like forever. It was surreal! By Che's suggestion, I called a friend because I didn't want to go home and be left in silence with only my thoughts and shock. This friend generously gave me her time and her support. She had a cup of tea for me, we prayed, and we talked. God ministered to me.

During my times of sickness, God opened our eyes to the truth that we were so blessed. And our stomachs! There's nothing like a meal to bring people together. So many people shared their love by cooking meals for us during times when I wasn't well. Their visits strengthened and nourished us. It was an exciting time to get to know people. Our marriage was strengthened as we spent time with other couples and talked about how we were staying strong. Talking about it made it real, and hearing other people's stories renewed our faith and encouraged us to go on in our faith.

Whenever I asked Che what would be most helpful to him during my times of illness, he said that it was having meals taken care of. So that's what we asked for. Not having to cook made his life easier and allowed him to navigate work, my medical visits, and the boys' extracurricular schedules. I couldn't ask for more help! This simple request helped us tremendously.

During these times, the blessings flowed in with great ease! God overwhelmed my heart and home with His sweet aroma through the fragrance of food. My cup ran over and we were never in want. At just the right time, the doorbell always rang and there was someone at my door or a gift certificate in the mailbox to provide a meal. We sometimes had too much.

This helped Che and I focus on us. God gave in abundance! Life was good.

Asking for help relieved stress in our lives so that we didn't argue or have unnecessary disagreements. We knew the areas where we were limited and being stretched thin. We didn't have to do everything ourselves, as long as things got done. The support of loved ones prevented us from placing unrealistic expectations on one another. Asking for help left room for us to better relate to each other.

The greatest support we had was through prayer. We can't count the number of people who prayed for us through sickness and other difficult times we experienced. We aren't shy about sharing with trusted friends what we're going through, because we know that prayer works. We know that the enemy wants people to stop praying, so we refused to stop. We called people to pray for us every time we received bad news.

Being covered by prayer has been our lifeline. God has moved us through difficulty and kept our marriage strong not only because of our prayers, but because of the many people interceding on our behalf!

Fourteen
The Couple that Gives Each Other a Break

Some people fear being apart. They fear allowing each other to have different interests or hobbies. Che and I feel that pursuing our own interests brings strength to our marriage. We're secure enough in our relationship and with each other to give each other a break!

If Che gets to do what he likes apart from me, he returns to me a contented man. If I get to do what I like apart from Che, I return to him a contented woman. When we're together after breaks, we are both happy and fulfilled, wanting to be in each other's company. We treasure each other more.

Taking the time for myself and my interests, independent of Shireen, is important. It's not that I don't include her; it's that we give each other space to be included or not.

I have an introverted tendency, so I sometimes enjoy just watching TV alone. I also have my own group of friends that I've known since public school. I hang out with them on occasion and we ski together too. Sometimes it's boys-only, and other times we include our families. I give Shireen the same opportunity to have her own space.

I believe we can be together but still have some independence. Shireen and I are very secure in our relationship, so we don't feel threatened. We do things apart from each other, but not that often because she really is cute, and I love being around her all the time.

My husband was a warrior in my fight with cancer. He remained so strong and took on many roles. I called him *Driving Miss Daisy*, *Mr. Mom*, *Daddy Day Care*, and *Superman* all in one.

My heart is filled with a deep appreciation for him. My eyes still well with tears when I think about his love. He showed love to me consistently in so many practical ways.

I'm not sure who was more tired. He worked so hard inside and outside our home, making sure everything worked like a well-oiled machine. He deserved to have breaks; he needed them in order to keep up with the demands while I was sick.

Che continued his commitment to the gym even through my sickest moments. He continued his routine because it gave him physical strength and mental space. This was important to him. Although I didn't always like it, and couldn't figure out why he had to go so often or at the specific times he chose, I realized that it made him happy. I could feel his stress build when he didn't work out and could feel the ease at which he engaged with the rest of life when he did. What was important to him became important to me. He needed that outlet and I didn't begrudge him that. I may not have liked the times he chose to go, but I knew it was a necessity. I was also the beneficiary of the results. We were both blessed.

Many times, he quietly disappeared to the basement to get away and be by himself. He would watch his favourite shows or listen to his favourite tunes. We laugh a lot about how he escapes. He knows I know his secret! When I couldn't find him, I knew where he was and that he needed to be there. Afterward he would come back more attentive, more willing and with more patience.

He doesn't go far, but that act of going down to the basement, a space where he can be alone with his thoughts and feelings, builds him up. It is his own self-endorsed timeout. I have to appreciate it, accept it, and encourage it. Even Jesus took timeouts from the ones He loved to be by Himself. He was practicing a biblical principal.

Che also has gone away on ski trips, sometimes halfway around the world and for longer periods of time than I wished. Those trips haven't happened at the most convenient times, but I know that my sicknesses haven't been convenient either. If Che stayed home and missed those opportunities, he would not have been a rested and happy husband. He would have continued to take care of me, but he might have later resented doing so. Not getting space away from me, the children, and work would have been unhealthy for him and for us. I've needed to support Che in these trips, so that he knows how valued he is. Supporting Che to go even when I needed him meant putting his needs before my own, which was a sign of respect and appreciation on my part.

This is one of the most loving things she could have done for me. Letting me go on these trips has given me permission to live in my happy place without guilt. It has allowed me to regain some control of my life, to focus on myself. Self-care is important.

In a marriage, especially in difficult times, it's very important to take the time to distance yourself from the problem, both physically and emotionally. It's hard to take care of someone else if you aren't taking care of yourself. It's hard to be strong without strengthening yourself.

> In a marriage, especially in difficult times, it's very important to take the time to distance yourself from the problem, both physically and emotionally.

In my state of illness, taking time away was much easier for me. I was forced away from a lot of things! But what I appreciated is that Che would take the boys on excursions after making sure I had everything I needed to be comfortable. There were times when everyone was home, and I was just given time to worship or be sad. Che gave me space and helped me navigate space from my boys, so they wouldn't be insulted when mommy needed to be alone.

I'm thankful that even before getting sick, we practiced giving each other space. We were mindful of each other and what our needs were, not feeling insulted by the other wanting to take time away. This has taken some getting used to, as the timing hasn't always been convenient, but the results in how rich our relationship and communication has become is proof that it's a necessity.

Be completely humble and gentle; be patient, bearing with one another in love. (Ephesians 4:2)

Fifteen
The Couple that Lives Life as Normal

The people around us often didn't know when we were suffering through various problems—and that's because during our most difficult times we continued to live life with joy. Life didn't come to a stop just because of challenges. In fact, the challenges probably allowed us to enjoy the good times even more than we otherwise would have.

When I was in labour with my second son, I went to the hospital the Sunday morning he was due. I wasn't ready to stay or be admitted, so they sent me home and told me I would be back later that evening. Instead of going home, I went straight from the hospital to church. Why not? I had no idea when we would return to church again, and I wanted our routine to continue. I'm so glad we went to church that morning since I later laboured two days straight. The delivery ended up being by C-section and left me in the hospital for a week.

On another Sunday morning—Mother's Day, in fact—the day after I had my first miscarriage, I went to church. I had my second miscarriage while I was at a training conference and visiting Che's family in London, Ontario. Afterward I stayed at the conference, and Che and I even had dinner that night with his family. But Che knew when I needed to rest and excuse myself, and we worked together to make sure no one knew what was happening. We didn't want to ruin a good visit.

Our most difficult hurdle was cancer. While going through it, I didn't look like or act like a cancer patient. As well as being a teacher, I'm also a pastor. I continued making life as normal as possible. I taught and I preached after surgeries and led worship after chemo. I even performed a wedding!

The day of my last radiation treatment, we went to a family reunion and I danced late into the night. We had left the hospital earlier that day, focused on the fun we were going to have with our family. That evening became a celebration.

Throughout my three years of being ill, the boys had continued with life as if nothing was happening. Their school wasn't affected and their grades didn't change. Their extracurricular activities didn't change. Che went to their events, and I got to hear the play-by-play after. We enjoyed attending church as usual.

We celebrated every occasion we could, such as birthdays and Thanksgiving, Christmas and Easter. We still remembered and planned for Mother's Day, Father's Day, and anniversaries. We went out for date nights when we could, even if they looked different. We ate meals together as a family, even if I wasn't eating or couldn't stay long at the table. We continued praying as a family, even though the boys met me in our bedroom instead of theirs.

Our setbacks hit us at the most inopportune times, and we decided that we wouldn't freeze in fear and watch life pass us by and then live in regret. Rather, we would forge ahead despite it all. I needed to do that. Living in the moment strengthened me to live for the future.

Not everyone could do what we did. Sometimes my husband thought I was crazy, like when I preached the week after having surgery for cancer, or when I performed a wedding while suffering the side effects of chemo. But he also supported my desire to keep things as normal as possible and focus on the good. We wanted to continue creating happy memories for our family.

When Che needed to put boundaries around me—for my own good, out of love—I knew that he was looking out for my best interest. In these times, we considered what we were doing and planned to take rests. But together we did everything we could to keep up the status quo, and this was the best decision we could ever have made. It showed our boys how God gives us strength and works in our lives to keep us in a place of joy and peace even during difficulty.

Sixteen
The Couple that Celebrates Small Victories

Along a journey of challenges, one always has small victories. Every time we reached a milestone, we celebrated.

We celebrated when we got to the end of a difficult week. We celebrated when we didn't have a disagreement when we were tired. We celebrated when we successfully navigated a busy schedule, and everyone was where they needed to be at the right times. We celebrated when appointments were cancelled and we got to rest. We celebrated when meals were prepared on time and there were leftovers for lunch. We celebrated when we were working with a budget and we managed to buy groceries and everything we needed due to sales. We celebrated when we remembered our anniversaries or birthdays; we don't usually forget these things, but when you're going through a storm sometimes things get missed.

We talked about each other's days and the good things that happened in each day. If Che made a contact or new client, or if we accomplished our to-do lists, we celebrated.

I had surgeries two years in a row just before Christmas, and we celebrated the fact that I was able to come home and celebrate Christmas with the family. We celebrated that I was alive! If I walked to the bathroom or down the stairs on my own after a surgery, we celebrated. If I didn't have as much pain as the day before, we celebrated.

We celebrated getting to bed early or getting good sleep. When I was going through treatment, we celebrated Che making it through the week after taking care of most of the household responsibilities from early mornings to late evenings. We celebrated him going to chemo with me and being in the hospital without showing signs of stress or discomfort.

> The focus of our celebrations isn't on what isn't happening but on what was...

On our wedding anniversary in 2017, we celebrated me being well enough to go on a getaway and going out in public while bald. The focus on all our celebrations isn't on what *is* happening, but on what *was*. We made the choice to focus on the good, and we found something to celebrate every day.

Seventeen
The Couple that Keeps Romance and Intimacy Alive

Many waters cannot quench love; rivers cannot sweep it away. (Song of Solomon 8:7)

Before we were married, we heard the repeated advice to keep dating, even after marriage. We made a commitment to make sure we did. It's much easier said than done, especially after having children, but once the commitment is made it does happen.

We had to re-evaluate many times how we were going to make this a consistent pattern in our lives. Every season meant making adjustments to how our dating life was going to look, but we never stopped dating. We kept dating even while I was sick.

Intimacy isn't just about the physical. It's about knowing each

> Intimacy isn't just about the physical. It's about knowing each other in every way, without hiding or hesitation.

other in every way, without hiding or hesitation. With tubes sticking out of each side of my body, and sores in my mouth and various other places, with my stomach constantly sick and pain in my bones, with my hair falling out, I didn't feel attractive. I'm sure this is totally understandable. I didn't want to attract attention or affection. Intimacy was most often far from my mind, although very close to my heart.

> *How handsome you are, my beloved! Oh, how charming!* (Song of Solomon 1:16)

I wanted to make Che happy. I wanted to take care of his needs, and I needed to know that I was still enough for him. He never made me feel like I wasn't enough and he never pressured me for physical intimacy. But every man has needs—so do women—and sexual activity needs to be regular in every marriage. I needed him to know that although I often couldn't respond to him in a physical way, I was still attracted to him. My heart still desired him.

I chose to tell him this every chance I got. We made sexual advances through words, which kept life exciting. It allowed us to know that our physical love was still alive, just on hold.

Che always told me how beautiful I was to him. He winked at me and whispered sweet nothings in my ears. He told me when he thought I looked good. He complimented me all the time. He spoke to my insecurities and made me feel special. He wanted me to be happy.

We intentionally worked at building intimacy in our marriage during this season.

THE COUPLE THAT KEEPS ROMANCE AND INTIMACY ALIVE

Where and when we could, we carved out time for each other. This created the atmosphere for intimacy to occur. I never felt like my needs had been forgotten. I'm thankful for that.

You have stolen my heart, my sister, my bride; you have stolen my heart with one glance of your eyes... (Song of Solomon 4:9)

We created intimacy by stealing and sharing glances at each other from across a room, and sharing touches whenever we were with each other. Every touch was important. Both sexual and non-sexual touches expressed our love and kept us close.

Let him kiss me with the kisses of his mouth—for your love is more delightful than wine. (Song of Solomon 1:2)

Giving each other a kiss brought closeness. We looked forward to the good morning kisses, the welcome home kisses, and the goodbye kisses when Che left for work or I went in for surgery or treatment. These small actions carried more meaning than they had before.

Che liked to pat my bottom so much so that my youngest son still smiles at this gesture and tells me that his dad loves me.

He and I shared space. We dated by watching movies together on a laptop. Although walks were now doctor's orders, we thought of them as five-, ten-, or fifteen-minute dates. We took these opportunities to hold each other's hand and share our deepest thoughts and feelings—or just to share our love without any words at all. We took the time to treasure these walks and moments together.

When I gained strength and my pain lessened, I made a conscious effort to surprise Che and make more advances, so that he knew when I was ready for physical intimacy. After all he had done for me, it was a joy to be the one to add spice to our life and be romantic! He grew to love these surprises.

Eighteen
The Couple that Chooses Love

Our love wasn't made by the vows everyone witnessed the day we got married, even though they seemed so big at the time. Our love is made by the small choices we make every day. We chose each other the day of our wedding and have committed to choose *us* every day since.

We didn't have a choice when it came to the difficult circumstances we have had to live through, but we could choose each other moment by moment and day by day.

Through our words and actions, we continue to feed our love. Feeding our love fed our marriage. Our relationship didn't deteriorate through our difficult times; it grew. We grew as individuals. We grew as partners.

> *Dear children, let us not love with words or speech but with actions and in truth.* (1 John 3:18)

Our vows were made before the Lord. These spoken vows were promises to God. We started with Jesus at the centre of our relationship and knew that He would keep us from self-centeredness in the good or bad times. We couldn't be focused on Jesus and ourselves at the same time.

> *Love is patient, love is kind. It does not envy, it does not boast, it is not proud. It does not dishonor others, it is not self-seeking, it is not easily angered, it keeps no record of wrongs. Love does not delight in evil but rejoices with the truth. It always protects, always trusts, always hopes, always perseveres.* (1 Corinthians 13:4–7)

God's design for our marriage cannot be lived out on our own. We need God's help! It's a difficult task, but it's also the only way to have a healthy marriage. If we lean into His power and allow the Holy Spirit to give us what we need, it's possible to have happiness in hardship.

The passage of Scripture from 1 Corinthians really shows a picture of the love God has extended to us. With that love in us, we can love each other. Christ loved us in this way. We have received it, and when it fills us we are able to share it with each other.

Christ's love helped us to look at Him and not ourselves. Focusing on Jesus gave me and Che the perspective we needed to keep our love and marriage strong. Looking at Christ kept us from focusing on our problems, which added love to our marriage. Focusing on Jesus filled us with power to express our love in a positive way, even when life was hard. Our ability to love wasn't hard, but some situations were.

We weren't perfect, but our love was patient and kind, filled with moments when our needs were secondary to each other. Our love protected and grew trust. It hoped for better days and kept going. Putting these scriptures, and many more, into practice filled our marriage with peace and contentment during the storm of illness.

Christ's love helped us to think differently. We truly did spend a lot of time in prayer for each other and ourselves. Listening to Jesus truly did change our hearts and minds.

We couldn't spend time with the Lord and then not do what He said. Che was able to keep taking care of me because the love of God had filled his life. I was able to show appreciation for him and find ways to give him a break because I had spent so much time in prayer. This strengthened me and helped me to in turn strengthen Che.

Christ's love helped us to live the life of love our marriage needed, even through difficult seasons. It's easy to demonstrate love when life is easy and there isn't anything in the way to challenge the love we want to express to each other.

With His love, we were able to make the moments count. We didn't waste time in conflict or responding to sickness. We didn't want to lose any precious time that would steal from us the happiness in our marriage. Sickness was already stealing too much. With the atmosphere in our home filled with peace, love grew and contentment stayed. Peace brought healing—and that was our goal. We wanted me to be healed so we could continue enjoying our marriage.

> With the atmosphere in our home filled with peace, love grew and contentment stayed.

The love we had, the love that allowed us to say our vows, isn't the same love that kept our marriage strong through the difficult times. Life wasn't difficult when we got married. We didn't have to make any sacrifices at the time we said "I do."

> *Submit to one another out of reverence for Christ.*
>
> *Wives, submit yourselves to your own husbands as you do to the Lord. For the husband is the head of the wife as Christ is the head of the church, his body, of which he is the Savior. Now as the church submits to Christ, so also wives should submit to their husbands in everything.*
>
> *Husbands, love your wives, just as Christ loved the church and gave himself up for her… In this same way, husbands ought to love their wives as their own bodies. He who loves his wife loves himself… However, each one of you also must love his wife as he loves himself, and the wife must respect her husband.* (Ephesians 5:21–25, 28, 33)

The love that carries us through difficulties is the kind of love that reflects Christ's relationship with His Church. That kind of love can only come through daily prayer and the Holy Spirit giving us what we need. Che and I relied on that.

In our relationship, we needed to demonstrate mutual submission. We needed to give each other what was needed and not compare ourselves to each other. We needed to both be willing to go the extra mile. Even if that didn't end up happening, keeping that commitment and plan helped us navigate the hard moments.

Jesus went the extra mile for us, and we are to follow His example of love. In Scripture, the relationship between Jesus and the Church is compared to the marriage relationship. Jesus pours His mercy and love into our lives and we must pour it into each other. He asks us to lay down our lives for each other in love. Through prayer, He gives us the ability to do so.

> Jesus pours His mercy and love into our lives and we must pour it into each other.

I've always had the same answer when asked what advice I would give a husband as to what choices he should make in marriage. I say, "Obey Scripture."

I loved Shireen and I had to love her like Christ loves the Church. I love myself and knew I would give myself the best, so I had to give her the best. We were one, and how I treated Shireen reflected our unity.

If I wanted God to bless us and answer my prayers, I had to be right in the love I expressed to Shireen.

For me, how I choose to show love is simple. It may not always be easy to do, and we may not always be perfect at it, but the choice is easy: just obey God and do what the Scripture says.

I worked hard at showing Che respect. I took note of his actions and drew attention to them so that our boys would see that their father was showing practical love to them and me. It wasn't hard to find reasons to respect him and to let him know. As he followed Christ, I saw a strong and beautiful man whom I was proud to have as my husband.

We entered a covenant relationship the day we were married. We both had roles given to us in Scripture, but the purpose of those roles is to keep us unified. If Che or I were to focus on our unmet needs, or focus on our struggles instead of the Lord, our very union would struggle. In our difficulties, when my health was poor and our finances were in trouble, we didn't need to add any more struggle to our love.

God stands with us in marriage and is especially close in difficult times. He didn't abandon us. He kept His promise to never leave us or forsake us. Satan comes to kill, steal, and destroy, but we weren't going to allow those difficulties to kill our marriage, steal our love, or destroy our family.

> Satan comes to kill, steal, and destroy, but we weren't going to allow those difficulties to kill our marriage, steal our love, or destroy our family.

Whoever does not love does not know God, because God is love. (1 John 4:8)

My command is this: Love each other as I have loved you. Greater love has no one than this: to lay down one's life for one's friends. (John 15:12–13)

We know that our power to build a happy, successful marriage comes because of our trust in and relationship with Jesus. We are Christians. We love God. We invite Him into our struggles, confident that He gives us what we need to be examples of His love to each other. He helps us to find joy despite the circumstances we face. He helps us to separate our struggle from our love and fight the struggle together with love.

Our marriage hasn't been trouble-free, but we've always known that if we go to God together we will make it through the difficult journey together.

In our difficulties, we've had to continually die to our own wishes. The only way to live in love in marriage is to die to self.

> The only way to live in love in marriage is to die to self.

In sickness, I had few wishes. I wished to be well. I wished that I wasn't a burden. I wished to enjoy activities with my family. I wished to be pain-free. All these things kept me from serving and participating in life the way I wanted. I couldn't help being in my physical state.

As I watched Che, he had to give up a lot. His days were shaped by these illnesses. His time was not his own. His schedule worked around mine and our boys'. He had wishes that were totally different than mine, but he put those to the side or made them secondary. He didn't always get what he wanted. I didn't either, but I had no choice. He made a choice, one that reflected us instead of him.

Be devoted to one another in love. Honor one another above yourselves. (Romans 12:10)

Che was devoted to us. He was devoted to me. When asked about this, he always goes back to saying that he took his vows seriously.

Our love has been easy, but our life has often been hard! Knowing how much he loves me and how much I love him keeps us working to make the tough times seem weak against our strong love. Knowing how strong God's power is in our lives keeps us working at our marriage with enjoyment.

These aren't just words. We truly believe this and trust God. Whether or not it has felt good, we have chosen to continue to just apply God's Word to our marriage, and it has brought not only enjoyment but fulfillment. God's Word and way for marriage truly does work!

Above all, love each other deeply, because love covers over a multitude of sins. (1 Peter 4:8)

Therefore what God has joined together, let no one separate. (Mark 10:9)

I recently read an article online about a couple named Wanda and Marvin Brewington. By 2017, they had been married for 47 years and beaten cancer twice. But currently he was battling multiple sclerosis and she, Parkinson's disease. When they were asked about what kept them so happy and in love, they said that the secrets to a lasting marriage include "truth, honesty and not letting the small things get you down. But most of all never forgetting to laugh and have fun. It is hard work, but it has always been worth the work it takes."[1]

Even before reading this, Che and I had been practicing those very things. It seems to me that learning these secrets early in marriage, or maybe even earlier, truly keeps a marriage strong late into life.

Che has said many times that the *actions* of commitment follow the *thought* of commitment. His choices have always been made possible because of a thought pattern.

The struggles and challenges we've lived through haven't been easy. Although we've suffered many times in many ways, our marriage hasn't. We've remained happy and gotten stronger.

I am blessed with the most amazing man to have as a life partner. I don't know if our relationship is so easy because of our personalities or because of our choices. Maybe it's both.

Most certainly it is God! He has blessed us with favour as we have chosen to believe His Word and put Him first in our relationship. He has proven Himself through the joy and ease that we have in our marriage.

We have been asked many times how we were doing during the various struggles. We've been asked what our secret was or what we were doing to manage not having any major marital problems. We have only one reason for our success in marriage;

---

[1] Olivia Elgart, "For Richer for Poorer…," *Daily Mail*. December 7, 2017 (https://www.dailymail.co.uk/femail/article-5148843/Couple-married-47-years-goes-viral-glam-photoshoot.html).

we don't know what we have done to deserve such fulfillment and happiness. But we know that it is the grace of God at work in our lives. We have given our lives to God as we give our lives to each other. We have followed God's design for marriage and haven't compromised.

Marriage takes work. We both love our jobs, but we still must work to be successful in them. We've applied this same principle to our marriage. We love each other, but we still must work and do things that help us continue to enjoy our relationship. It's simple work, although it isn't always easy. The first work is obedience to God, and then the rest follows. This is especially true during seasons of hardship. We must keep obeying God without compromise. We must keep doing the things that bring life to our love and never forget our commitment to those things.

The couple that stays together through hard times…
Prays together
Laughs together
Cries together
Lives in the moment and doesn't ignore hardship
Has a support system
Gives each other a break
Lives life as normal
Keeps romance and intimacy alive
Celebrates small victories
And chooses love
To have and to hold from this day forward
For better or for worse
For richer or for poorer
In sickness and in health
To love and to cherish
Till death do they part.

In Closing

Throughout this book, Che and I shared our thoughts on what we believe it takes to keep a marriage strong during the seasons and storms of life. Through sharing a little of our own personal story and journey, we've also shared the lessons God has taught us… lessons that have worked to keep our marriage thriving.

We have been asked so many times, "How do you keep your relationship strong?" We've never felt that it took much or that it was hard. It has come easy for us through God's grace. But when we look at the actions and thoughts we are committed to, we've found that we have practiced certain things over and over until they've become natural habits and responses.

We've only been married for seventeen years, but during that time we have faced a lot of challenges. We've had miscarriages. We've lost jobs and gone through financial difficulty. We've lost family members. We've battled many sicknesses, including cancer.

Yet through these battles our relationship hasn't suffered. Why?

We have grown stronger. How?

We truly believe that God has blessed us and wants to use our relationship to help others. This blessing has come as a result of our obedience to Him. We have kept our vows and practiced tangible habits that have fed our marriage and brought honour to God.

We have learned that the secrets to a happy marriage actually aren't a secret at all. They aren't hidden, and they aren't mysterious. They're the result of small, deliberate choices that have made a big difference. God outlines clearly in Scripture what we are to do and how we are to treat each other. The main message is to put the other person's needs above your own and to cover your relationship in prayer.

God used these practices in our lives to keep us not just happy but fulfilled and utterly content with our marriage. We've focused on the goodness of God. We've let His love and strength fill our lives.

Life has been hard, but our marriage has been good. We wish the same for your marriage too.

About the Authors

Che and Shireen have been married for seventeen years. They have two beautiful teenaged boys. Che is self-employed and works in the film and television industry. Shireen is an ordained reverend with the Church of the Nazarene and has her own ministry, Connect3Ministries.

They are associates with Family Life Canada and together they assist churches in supporting marriages and trying to bring health and healing to them. They speak at retreats, provide resources and support, and train people to become marriage mentors. They themselves are marriage mentors. They enjoy doing life together and being used by God to help marriages become stronger.